A Memorandum of the
80th Illinois Volunteer Infantry:
Civil War Notes of Pvt. Armstrong McGee

A Memorandum of the 80th Illinois Volunteer Infantry: Civil War Notes of Pvt. Armstrong McGee

Edited by Joshua A. Claybourn

Claybourn Genealogical Society, Inc.
MMXIV

First Printing: 2014

ISBN 978-0-9906516-0-4

Claybourn Genealogical Society, Inc.
100 E. Jennings St.
Newburgh, IN 47630

www.Claybourn.org
cgs@claybourn.org

Contents

Preface

This work is a regimental log of the 80th Illinois Volunteer Infantry Regiment documenting its activities in the American Civil War from 27 October 1863 to 17 June 1865.

While the author's name is not included with the original, it was obtained from ancestors of Private Armstrong McGee, who served in Company G of the 80th Illinois. While the author cannot be determined conclusively, it is presumed to be Private McGee, a 5-foot 7-inch, red-headed 24-year-old farmer from Randolph County, Illinois.

There is no evidence that this memorandum has ever been published before, nor is there evidence that previous Civil War historians knew of its existence.

In copying this document the editor has endeavored to stay as true as possible to the original text. The original, handwritten document is structured like a journal with entries in chronological order. Some are longer entries written in complete sentences, while others are shorter, occasionally with just one or two words to note the weather that day.

In general the text of each entry is transcribed word for word and letter for letter, insofar as it is possible to render handwritten matter into existing typography. However, the editor has taken the liberty of re-punctuating and re-paragraphing throughout. By today's standards the author used far too little punctuation, particularly periods. For organizational ease the editor has also added breakpoints for each year.

Editorial intrusion has been kept to a minimum and is shown in italics within square brackets: [*editorial comment*]. Words that are not clearly legible are treated as follows: if unreadable, the matter in question will be represented within square brackets by the italicized word "illegible": [*illegible*]. If there is a good indication of what the unreadable word might be, the likely word is followed by an italicized question mark within square brackets: [*?*]. A passage that has been transcribed exactly as found in the original source, complete with any erroneous spelling or other nonstandard presentation, is immediately followed by the standard italicized "sic" within square brackets: [*sic*].

The 80th Illinois Volunteer Infantry Regiment saw substantial action in the war. It traveled over 6,000 miles and was engaged in more than 20 pitched battles. Although the language used in this memorandum is naturally choppy and rough compared to more modern narratives, it will hopefully serve as a useful puzzle piece in the larger history of the regiment, and indeed of the war itself.

1863

On or about the 20th of Oct. 1863 we moved from Battle Creek, Tenn. to Bridgeport, Ala. and was put in the 3rd Brigade, 3rd Division, 11th Army Corps. The 3rd Brigade was commanded by Col. Hecker of the 82nd Illinois, the 3rd Division by Gen. Schurz, and the 11th Army Corps. by Major General O.O. Howard. The 11th and 12th Corps. was there laying at Bridgeport preparing for an expedition to open communications to Chattanooga by a nearer route.

Oct. 27th. Packed up early in the morning and was ready to move at 6 o'clock with three days rations in our haversacks. Marched across the river and laid there one hour. We then marched 6 miles to Saltpeter Cave and stopped here ½ hour. Companies C, K, A, and I were left here to guard a gap. Our forces were divided here. The 11th Corps. took one road and the 12th the other. We then marched on until night. The 80th Ill. and the 68th N.Y. camped for the night in a small field.

Oct. 28th. Marched at sunrise until 9 o'clock. We then halted in an old camp ground for ½ hour. When the 80th Ill. and 68th N.Y. were sent ¾ of a mile to guard a gap in the mountains here we got our dinner. By the time dinner was over a regiment from the 12th Army Corps. came to relieve us. We then started toward Chattanooga, passed the 12th Army Corps, and 20 min to 3 o'clock we heard the sound of artillery on Lookout Mtn. We were then ordered to load. We went on a quick march from then until night. The enemy were shelling our troops as they passed Lookout Mountain. We passed their batteries a little before sundown. Co. D. had one man slightly wounded as we passed. We camped for the night in a corn field out of range of their batteries.

Oct. 29th. There was one Brigade of the 17th Army Corps. camped about two miles down the valley from the main force. Gen. Longstreet came to the conclusion that he would undertake to capture our train during the night and sent a force down the valley for that purpose and run into this Brigade. Our troops fought desperately for about an hour. The enemy was defeated and retired without accomplishing anything. We heard the pickets commence firing at half past 11. We moved down to the foot of a hill near Lookout Point and halted. Part of our troops charged the hill and took it. We then moved a little farther down the valley and halted and fixed bayonets so as to be ready to charge if they attacked us. We laid here an hour and a half or two hours. The 80th Illinois and 68th N.Y. was then ordered to go down where that brigade was. We got there at daylight. Companies B and H were put on picket. The other companies formed behind the railroad bank. The forces that were here were busy throwing up breastworks. The enemy soon planted two guns on a point on Lookout Mt. opposite to us and commenced shelling us but did not do much damage. Our loss was light. There was a great many battery horses killed in the night charge. The enemy's loss was heavier.

Oct. 30th. Done picket duty. Rained nearly all day.

Oct. 31st. Moved back ½ mile into the Mts.

Nov. 1st. Moved 200 yards into line. At 5 p.m. commenced throwing up entrenchments. Worked until midnight.

Nov. 2nd. Worked on the entrenchments.

Nov. 3rd. Worked on the entrenchments.

Nov. 4th. In camp.

Nov. 5th. In camp. Rained nearly all day.

Nov. 6th to 12th. In camp.

Nov. 13th. Moved ¼ mile nearer Lookout Mt.

Nov. 14th to 20th. In camp.

Nov. 20th. Had inspection at 9 a.m. Got orders to pack our knapsacks and have them ready to take to Headquarters in a moment's warning.

Nov. 21st. In camp.

Nov. 22nd. Got orders to be ready to march in a moment's notice. Took out knapsack to Brigade Headquarters. Left camp at half past one and marched to Chattanooga. Got into Chattanooga at half past 7. Camped for the night east of town.

Nov. 23rd. We had orders for no one to leave camp. Our troops commenced moving out at 12 a.m. They shortly became engaged with the enemy and took the first line of rifle splits. The 11th Army Corps. moved out at 3pm on the left flank and drove in the enemy's skirmishers. We laid in line of battle all night.

Nov. 24th. Company B went out reconnoitering at 3 o'clock and found the enemy in our front. The skirmishers commenced firing at daylight. The 80th had six men wounded. Henry Sees of Company B was among the number. He was severely wounded. The ball passed through both thighs. Private [*Edward*] Foster of Company G was also severely wounded. We advanced our line a short distance and threw up entrenchments. Lookout Mt. was taken.

Nov. 25th. The 11th Army Corps. moved 2 miles to the left and threw up entrenchments. Gen. Sherman crossed river on the night of the 24th and on the morning of the 25th engaged the enemy's left flank and took some important positions. Mission Ridge was taken.

Nov. 26th. Was waked up at 4 o'clock. Marched at half past 4. Went back to the river and crossed Chickamauga Creek and followed Braggs' retreating army until dark.

Nov. 27th. The army commenced moving at daylight. At [*illegible*] the 11th Army Corps. left the main army and marched to the left to get possession of a gap. Col. Hecker's brigade and part of Col. Smith's was sent to Red Clay Station to tear up the railroad track. We went out there and tore up the track and got back to where the Division was camped, about 12 o'clock at midnight. This was a hard day's march.

Nov. 28th. Moved back 4 miles to Corps. headquarters, near the gap, and went in camp. At 4 o'clock the 80th Ill. was sent back to help the train. Drew one day's rations.

Nov. 29th. Was ordered to be ready to march at 5 o'clock. Marched until 10 o'clock and then stopped one hour for dinner. Then marched to Cleveland and camped here. Overnight distance 18 miles.

Nov. 30th. Moved to Charleston, Tenn. 11 miles.

Dec. 1st. Moved to Athens. 15 miles.

Dec. 2nd. Moved 21 miles. Stopped at Sweetwater for dinner. Camped for the night near Philadelphia. Our advance had a slight skirmish with the Rebels in Philadelphia.

Dec. 3rd. Marched to Loudon 4 miles. The enemy left part of their wounded here and left 4 trains of cars in the river. We captured some meal and flour here and issued it out among the troops.

Dec. 4th. Was ordered to be ready to march at 8 a.m. At 9 we moved down to the river and laid there all day. Part of the 82nd Ill. crossed the river on flatboats and returned at sundown. Think it was done to deceive the enemy.

Dec. 5th. Was ordered to be ready to march at 1 o'clock in the morning. Went 5 miles over the river and crossed on a temporary foot bridge. Marched 20 miles and went in camp near Louisville, Tenn.

Dec. 6th. In camp. Received news of Longstreet's defeat at Knoxville.

Dec. 7th. Marched back to Philadelphia 21 miles. Our brigade was separated from the balance of troops. We were sent in advance.

Dec. 8th. Moved to Athens. 20 miles.

Dec. 9th. Moved to Charleston 15 miles and crossed the river on a raft.

Dec. 10th. In camp and worked on the railroad bridge.

Dec. 11th to 14th. In camp. The balance of the troops came up.

Dec. 15th. Marched to Cleveland 11 miles.

Dec. 16th. Moved 15 miles and went in camp. About the time we got our wood and made the fires we received orders to go 5 miles farther. Our General tried to get the order countermanded but did not succeed. Soon after we started it commenced raining and came down in torrents, and it was as dark as pitch. We had a jolly time marching that 5 miles. It took us till nearly midnight.

Dec. 17th. Marched to Lookout Valley 15 miles and camped on our old campground.

Dec. 18th to 21st. In camp. Weather cold.

Dec. 22nd. Relieved from duty in the 11th Army Corps.

Dec. 23rd. In camp and received clothing.

Dec. 24th. Moved to Whiteside Station 10 miles and put in the 3rd Brigade, 1st Division, 4th Army Corps. The brigade was commanded by Col. Grose, division by Gen. Stanley, Corps. by Granger.

Dec. 25th. Companies B and G moved up in the mountains north of the station. We packed up comfortable quarters and was in camp until Jan. 27th, 1864. We had plenty of wood handy, but had to carry most of our rations up the mountains.

1864

Jan. 27th. Moved down the Mt. before daylight and joined the regiment. Lieut. Colonel Wm. Kilgore of the 75th Ill. was put in command of the regiment. We marched to the foot of Lookout Mt. 11 miles and camped for the night.

Jan. 28th. Moved to the east side of Lookout Mt. 2 miles and went in camp.

Jan. 29th. Marched 11 miles. Camped near Tyner Station.

Jan. 30th to Feb. 2nd. In camp.

Feb. 2nd. Marched 12 miles and camped for the night within 8 miles of Cleveland.

Feb. 3rd. Marched 14 miles and camped within 5 miles of Charleston.

Feb. 4th. Turned back. Marched 7 miles. Camped near Cleveland. Company B was front on picket.

Feb. 5th. Marched 5 miles. Went in camp near Alltawah [*it is not clear which town the author is referring to, but it may have been Ooltewah*].

Feb. 6th. Marched to Blue Springs 3 miles and went in camp and was in camp until the 13th.

Feb. 13th. Went out on a scout. Returned to camp the same day.

Feb. 22nd. Marched to Red Clay Station from the Blue Springs. Our brigade was sent out to reconnoiter. We went 2 miles south. Then returned to the station. We came across a squad of rebels and captured one or two.

Feb. 23rd. Left Red Clay Station at two o'clock and marched to within 3 miles of Ringgold. We did not get into camp until about 9 o'clock.

Feb. 24th. Left camp at 8 a.m. Marched to within 4 miles of Dalton. Our cavalry skirmished with the rebels.

Feb. 25th. Skirmishing commenced soon after daylight. We formed in line of battle and built kind of a barricade with old logs. Co. A was thrown out as skirmishers. We advanced our lines between 9 and 10 o'clock and drove in the enemy's skirmishers. At 12m [*noon*] Company B relieved Company A and at sundown Company B was relieved by Company F. Our troops commenced moving back about 9 o'clock and moved back about 8 miles. We had 3 men wounded: John M. Holland of Company B in the left arm, Sgt. Criley of Company A in the knee, and Sgt. Joblin of Company C.

Feb. 26th. Soon after sunrise we formed our lines on a range of hills in our front. The enemy's cavalry soon came up and attempted to drive in our pickets. Sgt. Millbourn was slightly wounded. At 2 o'clock our forces all moved back 2.5 miles, excepting the 80th and the cavalry. We were relieved at 9 p.m. and moved back to within 3 miles of Ringgold.

Feb. 27th. Our Div. [?] the first started for Cleveland, Tenn. at 1 p.m. The 3rd brigade was in the advance. We camped within 13 miles of Cleveland. Gen. Forrest's cavalry attacked our train but did not do any harm.

Feb. 29th. Marched to Blue Springs and camped on the 30th Ind.'s old campground.

April 7th. Went out on a scout. Left camp at 3 p.m. and returned at 7 p.m. Was in camp until the 3rd of May when we started on the spring campaign.

May 3rd. Started at 12m [*noon*] and marched to Red Clay station 8 miles.

May 4th. Moved to Catoosa Springs.

May 5th. Moved ¼ of a mile onto a range of hills and threw up breastworks.

May 6th. In camp.

May 7th. Marched to Tunnel Hill. Our troops skirmished some with the rebels. We camped for the night on Tunnel Hill.

May 8th. Moved onto the rebels and made a big show in general. Out skirmishers were engaged all day.

May 9th. Laid in line of battle nearly all day. Moved ½ mile farther down the valley. Our skirmishers were engaged nearly all day. There was some cannonading.

May 10th. Skirmishing all day. There was considerable cannonading. We moved ¼ mile up the railroad.

May 11th. The skirmishers kept firing nearly all day. At 3 p.m. 8 companies of the 80th went on picket.

May 12th. Our brigade moved in front of the gap. The pickets kept firing all day and there was also some cannonading.

May 13th. The rebels evacuated their works during the night. We followed them up until night. Our advance skirmished with their rear guard all day.

May 14th. Moved 3 or 4 miles southeast. Found the enemy in their works near Resaca. About noon there was right heavy skirmishing and cannonading until about 4 o'clock when the enemy made a charge on our right flank and came very near driving it back. The 80th had 4 men wounded. William Jones of Company B was wounded in the left arm. Mark Miller of Company K in the leg. The other belonged to Companies D and G.

May 15th. Hard fighting at different times through the day. Gen. Hooker made a charge on the enemy's right and took his line of works with 4 pieces of artillery. The rebels made several charges during the night but were repulsed.

May 16th. Gen. [*Joseph*] Johnston evacuated during the night. We followed him across the river at Resaca and went 5 miles south of Resaca. The cars came up before we got across the river.

May 17th. Left camp at 9 a.m. Went through Calhoun. Marched 8 miles. Our advance had a right smart skirmish with the rebels near Adairsville.

May 18th. Went through Adairsville. Marched 6 miles.

May 19th. Left camp at 6 a.m. Marched through Kingston at 9 a.m. Skirmished with the rebels from Kingston to Cassville, Georgia.

May 20th to 22nd. In camp.

May 23rd. Left camp at 1 p.m. and crossed Etowah River. Marched 8 miles.

May 24th. Left camp at 6 a.m. and marched 7 miles.

May 25th. Left camp half past 9 a.m. and marched until sundown. The 20th Corps. was in the advance. They commenced skirmishing with the rebels on Pumpkinvine Creek. Gen. Hooker made several charges and lost heavy.

May 26th. We moved out in line early in the morning and threw up barricade. Our regiment was in the skirmish line. The 80th had 1 man killed and 3 wounded.

May 27th. Was relieved at 4 a.m. Moved ½ mile to the left. Formed a new line and built breastworks. Michael McLane with Company B was wounded. He had his left leg broken.

May 29th. Slight skirmishing all day. The rebels made several charges in the night but were repulsed.

May 30th. The skirmishers kept firing all day.

June 1st. Moved into the first line of pitts and relieved the 77th Pennsylvania. The skirmishers kept firing all day.

June 2nd. Laid in the rifle pitts. J. Woods of Company K and one of Company F was killed.

June 3rd. Laid in the rifle pitts. William Diamond of Company B was wounded.

June 4th. Company B was on the skirmish line. The 59th and 80th Illinois, 77th Pennsylvania, and 30th Indiana moved ¼ miles across the hollow to the left.

June 5th. The rebels evacuated during the night. They were all gone in the morning excepting a few cavalry. We laid in camp all day.

June 6th. Left camp a little after sunrise. Marched to within 3 miles of Ackworth, then went into camp.

June 7th, 8th and 9th. In camp. Cleaned up the camp, groomed, and had orders to have 5 roll calls and 2 dress parades a day.

June 10th. Left camp at 7 a.m. and advanced up to within ¾ miles from the enemy's works on Pine Knob and built breastworks.

June 11th. Finished our works in the evening. Our men formed a line 100 yards in advance of us and built works.

June 12th and 13th. Laid behind our works.

June 14th. At 5 p.m. the 80th and 84th Illinois and 77th Pennsylvania moved ½ mile to the left. Company B went on picket.

June 15th. The rebels evacuated their works in our front during the night and moved back over a mile. We followed them up and maneuvered around nearly all day and in the evening formed our lines and built works.

June 16th. Finished our works in the evening. Col. Grose advanced the 2nd line 150 yards in front of us.

June 17th. The enemy evacuated his works before daylight and moved back ¾ miles. Stanley's division, the 1st, was left in the reserve.

June 18th. We were in the reserve. There was very heavy skirmishing and cannonading in our front all day.

June 19th. The enemy evacuated their works before daylight and moved back over a mile. The 80th and 84th Illinois and the 9th and 36th Indiana were in the front line. Company D [?] had one man killed and 7 wounded. Benjamin Hawkins of Company K was killed. We advanced after dark and built works and worked on them until 12 o'clock.

June 20th. Company B did the skirmishing and had 2 men wounded, Sgt. Jacob Yant and Frederick Ricemann. Company A had 1 wounded. We were relieved at dark by the 77th Pennsylvania and at 8 a.m. part of our Brigade was relieved by the 14th Army Corps. We then moved back to the rear.

June 21st. At half past 1 p.m. five regiments moved ¾ miles to the right to support Grant's [?] Brigade. Company G had 4 more wounded by a shell.

June 22nd. Leroy [?] was wounded at daylight by a minnie ball. At 6 p.m. we moved to the right and relieved part of the 20th Army Corps. The 80th was in the second line. We built works.

June 23rd. We laid behind our works. Company F had 1 man wounded.

June 24th. Laid in our works.

June 25th. Company B and part of G was on the skirmish line.

June 26th. Laid in our works.

June 27th. Moved in the first line at half past 5 o'clock a.m. and relieved some of Gen. Grant's [?] men. Part of the first and second divisions charged the enemy's works but were repulsed. Our loss was pretty heavy. The 80th had two men killed and two wounded. Capt. Cunningham was slightly wounded in the leg. Jeff Davis of the 14th Army Corps. also charged the enemy's works but did not have much better success than we did.

June 28th. Laid behind our works.

June 29th. Behind our works.

June 30th. At dusk relieved the 75th Illinois on the first line.

July 1st. Behind our works.

July 2nd. The rebels shelled us a while before dark. After dark, moved about 300 yards to the left.

July 3rd. The rebels evacuated during the night. We followed them up at sunrise and found them in works 16 miles this side of Atlanta. Our advance skirmished with the rebels at different times through the day.

July 4th. Col. Grose's brigade charged across an open field on the enemy's skirmish pitts. We took them and then built a strong line of works. The 80th had one man killed 14 wounded. Alfred Cummings of Company B was mortally wounded.

July 5th. The rebels evacuated during the night. We followed them up early the next morning. The 1st division was in the rear.

July 6th. Went in camp.

July 7th, 8th and 9th. In camp.

July 10th. Moved 2 or 3 miles up the river.

July 11th. In camp.

July 12th. Crossed the river on pontoons and moved down the river to the right of Schofield's troops.

July 13th to 17th. In camp.

July 18th. Moved 4 miles northeast. Our brigade was in the rear.

July 19th. Advanced about 4 miles. Grose's brigade done some skirmishing.

July 20th. Advanced upon the enemy. Moved about 2 miles. Skirmished some with the rebels. Grose's brigade captured about 100 prisoners.

July 21st. Strengthened our line. The right of our brigade advanced their lines.

July 22nd. The rebels evacuated their works during the night. Our brigade started in pursuit of them. Before daylight we found them in their works near Atlanta. The 75th Illinois, 80th Illinois, and 30th Indiana went into camp. The balance of the brigade formed a line and built works. The enemy attacked McPherson's troops. McPherson was killed. The rebel loss was heavy. Our troops were victorious.

July 23rd, 24th and 25th. In camp.

July 26th. At 9 p.m. we moved into the front line and relieved part of the first brigade. McPherson's troops moved around to the right wing.

July 27th. Fixed up camp. There was some artillery firing.

July 28th. In camp. Heavy fighting on the right wing. McPherson's troops again engaged. Major Gen. O.O. Howard in command. Our troops again victorious. Rebel loss heavy.

July 29th. Considerable firing on the skirmish line. Isaac Sherfy of Company H and James Marlin of D wounded.

July 30th and 31st. In camp.

Aug. 1st. The 2rd Army Corps. moved around to the right wing.

Aug. 2nd. In camp. The skirmishers kept firing all day.

Aug. 3rd. The first and third division made a feint attack and drove in the enemy's skirmishers. Our brigade took 52 prisoners. Sam Corbitt of Company E and Rufus Cox of Company H were wounded.

Aug. 4th. In camp. Our skirmishers kept firing all day.

Aug. 5th. Our skirmishers made another assault upon the enemy's skirmish line. They succeeded in driving them a short distance but soon ran into concealed pitts. We lost heavy in killed and wounded. The 77th Pennsylvania had about half of their skirmishers either killed or wounded. The 80th had one man killed and one wounded. Eli Sanders of Company H was killed and Francis Foster of Company B was mortally wounded.

Aug. 6th and 7th. The skirmishers kept firing. There was also considerable cannonading.

Aug. 8th. There was two companies of the 80th out supporting the skirmish line.

Aug. 9th to 15th. In camp. Nothing of importance took place. Skirmishers kept firing and there was more or less cannonading every day.

Aug. 16th. The 59th Illinois exchanged brigades with the 84th Indiana. The 59th went in the Second Brigade, 3rd Division.

Aug. 17th. Our men made a feint movement on the left.

Aug. 18th. Our skirmishers made a demonstration in our front. They advanced up in the timber and fell back in their old line at dark.

Aug. 19th. Gen. Grose's made a feint attack with 4 or 5 regiments of his brigade.

Aug. 20th. The 9th and 36th Indiana, and 75th and 80th Illinois from our brigade and part of the 2nd brigade went out on a scout. We left camp at 3 a.m. and went out on our left wing and went about one mile east of the Augusta Railroad. We drove the enemy's pickets in and had a right smart skirmish. They were in McPherson's old works. We skirmished with them about an hour then returned to camp. Company A had 2 men wounded, 1 severely the other slightly. The 9th Indiana lost several men. John M. Holland came to the regiment.

Aug. 21st. In camp. All quiet.

Aug. 22nd. In camp. Got notice of the death of Francis Foster. He died at Vining Station on the 10th from the effect of his wound.

Aug. 23rd. Nothing of importance took place. James B. Newman got back from Bridgeport.

Aug. 24th. In camp.

Aug. 25th. Got orders to be ready to march at dark. Started a little after dark and moved toward the right. Marched very slow until 2 o'clock and then camped until morning.

Aug. 26th. The rebels commenced shelling us at sunrise but did not do much harm. We started about 9 o'clock a.m. and marched to the right. Marched about ten miles and camped for the night.

Aug. 27th. Left camp about half past 9 a.m. and marched until 1 p.m. Moved 4 miles. The 80th Ill. was sent out to protect the flank.

Aug. 28th. Left camp at half past one and marched until night.

Aug. 29th. In camp. Built works. Part of our troops was [sic] tearing up and burning the Montgomery Railroad.

Aug. 30th. Left camp at 8 a.m. Marched very slow. Went about 4 miles nearly east. One man of the 84th Ind. was wounded in the foot.

Aug. 31st. Left camp at 8 a.m. About 10 a.m. we came across the enemy in their works. We took the line without any loss. We ate our dinners and then marched 1 mile farther and went in camp and fortified.

Sept. 1st. Left camp at 7 a.m. and marched to the railroad and commenced tearing up the track. We burnt the ties and bent the rails. We tore up the track to within 2 miles of Jonesboro. About 4 p.m. the 14th Army Corps. engaged the enemy. We advanced to the scene of action and moved up to within 150 yards of the enemy's works and had a right smart skirmish. We built kind of a barricade. Orderly Sgt. Weyrick of Company C was slightly wounded in the hand. One man of Company H was also wounded. Jeff Davis's division of the 14th Army Corps. charged the enemy's works and took 8 pieces of artillery and a number of prisoners. If night had not come on so soon we would have made a pretty good haul there.

Sept. 2nd. The enemy evacuated during the night. We drew rations and then followed them up. Found them in works at Lovejoy Station. We then formed our lines and drove in their skirmishers. The rebels used 2 pieces of artillery on our brigade. Our regiment had 2 men killed and 3 wounded. Sgt. J. Ellis of Company H and H. McKinney of Company A was killed. Sgt. Barnes of Company G,

John Moore of Company F, and J. Duncan of Company A were wounded. The 80th was in the 2nd line.

Sept. 3rd. Finished our works. Our men got some artillery on the line and commenced shelling the enemy.

Sept. 4th. All quiet except skirmishing.

Sept. 5th. Commenced falling back after dark. The night was very dark and the roads muddy. Fell back to Jonesboro.

Sept. 6th. Moved to our old works at daylight.

Sept. 7th. Started back for Atlanta at 7 a.m. March 10 miles.

Sept. 8th. Left camp soon after daylight and marched to Atlanta. Went in camp southeast of town.

Sept. 16th. Edward Weaver came to the company.

Sept. 19th. Our div. went out at 2 p.m. for inspection. Gen. Stanley inspected us.

Sept. 20th. Lieut. J. H. Smith went to the hospital.

Sept. 23rd. Received orders to be ready to march at 12m [*noon*] with 2 days rations. Went out to guard a forage train. Went 15 miles and then camped for the night.

Sept. 24th. Started at daylight. Marched 5 or 6 miles then loaded our train and came back as far as Peach Tree Creek and camped for the night.

Sept. 25th. Went into camp about 11 a.m.

Sept. 26th. Sgt. A. G. Clifford started home on a furlough.

Sept. 30th. Presentation of division and brigade flags by Gen. Stanley at 2 p.m. and inspection.

Oct. 3rd. Packed up and was ready to march at daylight. Marched to within 4 miles of Marietta and went in camp.

Oct. 4th. Received orders at 9 a.m. to clean up camp. At 12m [*noon*] received orders to march immediately. Marched to Kenesaw Mt. and camped for the night. When we arrived in Marietta it was reported that the rebels held part of Kenesaw Mt. but we found it to be a mistake.

Oct. 5th. Drew two days rations and then started and moved very slow. The rebels were reported to be near. We advanced cautiously on Pine Knob. Went into camp on a small hill near Pine Knob. The rebels attacked our forces at Altoona [?] Station but were repulsed. They had a right sharp fight and came very near taking the place.

Oct. 6th. In camp. The 23rd Army Corps. passed us.

Oct. 7th. In camp. There was great many interesting rumors afloat.

Oct. 8th. Left camp at 3 p.m. Marched to within 1 ½ miles of Ackworth. We got in camp about 8 p.m.

Oct. 9th. At 3 p.m. moved ½ mile into a point of timber and went into camp.

Oct. 10th. Left camp about 3 p.m. Marched to within 1 ½ miles of Cartersville. Got into camp at half past 8 p.m. Marched 11 miles.

Oct. 11th. Left camp at daylight. Marched 14 miles and went in camp 1 mile south of Kingston.

Oct. 12th. Marched to within 2 miles of Rome. We got in camp about 10 p.m.

Oct. 13th. Left camp at 3 p.m. Marched 8 miles and then camped for the night. Half past 11 p.m. when we got in camp.

Oct. 14th. Left camp at daylight. Marched through Resaca. Went in camp 2 miles north of Resaca.

Oct. 15th. Left camp at sunrise and marched to Snake Creek Gap. Our brigade crossed Jones' Mts. We got on a high point near Snake Creek Gap and built kind of barricades [sic]. We could see the rebels passing up the gap below us. Companies B and F, and I Company of the 30th Indiana, were sent down to the gap to pick up stragglers but we got down too late. The advance of the 16th Army Corps. was just passing up the gap as we got down.

Oct. 16th. Drew rations and then marched 7 miles and went into camp.

Oct. 17th. Laid in camp and drew one day's rations.

Oct. 18th. Left camp at daylight and marched to within 6 miles of Summerville. Our brigade was in the advance.

Oct. 19th. Left camp at daylight and marched to Summerville.

Oct. 20th. Left camp a little after sunrise and marched to within ½ mile of Gaylesville, Alabama.

Oct. 21st, 22nd and 23rd. In camp. There was a parade detail sent out every day to forage but they did not get much.

Oct. 24th. Moved ¾ miles and then went into regular camp.

Oct. 25th and 26th. In camp.

Oct. 27th. Received orders at daylight to be ready to march at 8 a.m. Marched to Alpine 13 miles. Roads very muddy.

Oct. 28th. Left camp at 6 a.m. Marched to Lafayette 22 miles.

Oct. 29th. Left camp a little after sunrise and marched to Rossville 21 miles.

Oct. 30th. Marched to Chattanooga and then back to the foot of Lookout Mt. and went into camp.

Oct. 31st. Received order to be ready to march at an early hour. Went up to Chattanooga at 10 a.m. and got on the cars. The train started out at 2 p.m. and we arrived at Athens, Alabama. The next morning at daylight the troops that were stationed here got scared and left the evening before. It was reported that Forrest was advancing on the place. He did not come. There was one battalion each of the 73rd Indiana and 151st Ohio here to garrison the place.

Nov. 1st. We arrived at Athens at daylight and went out to the fort south of town.

Nov. 2nd. Started at daylight and marched to Elkton, Tennessee 21 miles. We forded Elk River. The roads were very muddy.

Nov. 3rd. Marched to Pulaski 15 miles. Rained nearly all day.

Nov. 4th to 23rd. In camp. We built comfortable quarters. The weather was very changeable. We had some right cold weather.

Nov. 23rd. Got orders to march at 12m [*noon*]. We moved across the pike onto a hill northwest of town and went into camp for the night. Our brigade was left in the rear.

Nov. 24th. Started at midnight and marched to Columbia 29 miles. We marched in rear of the train. We had a hard days march. We did not get into camp until after dark.

Nov. 25th. Moved out on line and built works. A little after dark we got orders to move and moved around to the west side of town. There was considerable firing on the skirmishline all day.

Nov. 26th. At half past 12m [*noon*] we moved ½ miles to the left and built kind of a barricade in front of the regiment. There was considerable firing on the skirmishline. We got orders at dark to be ready to move in a moment's warning but somehow did not move.

Nov. 27th. There was not as much skirmish firing as there was the day before. We got orders at dark to be ready to move in a moment's warning. We crossed the river and then went into camp. Very bad marching.

Nov. 28th. Formed a line near the river and built works. There was some skirmishing and cannonading through the day.

Nov. 29th. At 9 a.m. we moved back ¾ miles onto a range of hills and built works. We then got orders to march after dark. We were delayed a long while crossing a creek. The rebels came very near cutting part of our army off at Spring Hill. We could see their camp as we passed. It was within ¾ miles of the pike.

Nov. 30th. Arrived at Franklin about 10 a.m. We formed our lines and built temporary works. The rebel's cavalry made a dash upon our train about 2 a.m. and destroyed 25 wagons. They made another dash upon it at daylight but did not accomplish anything. Hood formed his line and commenced the attack about 4 p.m. Our regiment was on the 2nd line as soon as they commenced skirmishing. We commenced strengthening our works. The rebels made charge after charge. Our regiment was called on to support a battery. The fighting ceased at half past 9 p.m. They only succeeded in breaking our line at one place and did not hold that long. Our loss was light. Theirs was pretty heavy. We commenced evacuating our works at 10 p.m. Our rear guard left about 1 in the morning. We had to cross the river on one pontoon and it was rather slow crossing.

Dec. 1st. Arrived at Brentwood Station at sunrise and stopped one hour for breakfast. Got to Nashville about 1 p.m. We were all tired and sleepy.

Dec. 2nd. Commenced forming our lines at 12 p.m. Formed our lines and commenced building works. Got our works about half done when we got orders to be ready to march immediately. We then moved back on line with Fort Gillem. We commenced building breastworks about dark and worked until midnight. There was some slight skirmishing in our front.

Dec. 3rd. Finished our works. There was some firing on the skirmish line.

Dec. 4th and 5th. In camp. There was some firing on the skirmish line and some cannonading.

Dec. 6th. The 80th went on picket. Weather very cold.

Dec. 7th. The 77th Pennsylvania was on picket. The rebels charged on our skirmish line and drove it back ¼ mile. Our men turned upon them and drove them back a short distance at 4 p.m. Gen. Grose took the 9th Indiana and two pieces of artillery out and shelled the rebels out of our skirmish pitts. The 77th Pennsylvania had 2 men killed and 1 wounded.

Dec. 8th to 12th. In camp. Nothing of importance took place.

Dec. 13th. The 80th was on picket.

Dec. 14th. In camp. Weather moderated. The ground thawed out. Roads muddy.

Dec. 15th. Marched at 6 a.m. Moved to the right of Hillsboro and Hardin pikes. We kept moving up on them a short distance at a time until about 4 p.m. when there was a charge made and their lines broken. Our brigade captured several pieces of artillery and a number of prisoners. We moved down their lines as far as Granny White Pike when we had to stop on account of the darkness of the night. There was 18 pieces of artillery and 1200 prisoners captured during the day. Dillon wounded in the thigh. Scott E. on the right breast.

Dec. 16th. We commenced reconnoitering and forming our lines at sunrise. We found the enemy in position on the Franklin Pike about 5 miles south of town with their left resting on a range of hills. They had strong works. Our regiment was in the rear line. Gen. A.J. Smith broke their lines between 3 and 4 o'clock. We then charged along the whole line. The rebels were routed. We captured 30 pieces of artillery and 5000 prisoners. We followed them up until darkness set in.

Dec. 17th. Went in pursuit of the enemy. Went to Franklin where we had to stop and bridge the river. The 9th Indiana and the prisoners of the brigade worked on the bridge all night. Our cavalry pressed them close. They captured 3 pieces of artillery and quite a number of prisoners.

Dec. 18th. Marched to within 8 miles of Columbia.

Dec. 19th. Marched about 3 miles to a small river where we went in camp. Our regiment worked at the river until about 10 o'clock trying to float a raft across. We had two men drowned, J. Mackey of Company F and R. Wilson of Company I.

Dec. 20th. Built a bridge across the river and crossed and marched to the river opposite Columbia and then went in to camp.

Dec. 21st. In camp.

Dec. 22nd. Crossed the river and moved 1 ½ mile.

Dec. 23rd. Moved 5 miles.

Dec. 24th. Moved 14 miles. Camped 2 miles south of Linville.

Dec. 25th. Moved 15 miles. Rained in the afternoon. Roads very muddy. Passed through Pulaski, Tennessee.

Dec. 26th. In camp. Drew 3 days rations to last 5.

Dec. 27th. Moved 12 miles. Roads very muddy. Rained.

Dec. 28th. Moved to Lexington, Alabama. 10 miles.

Dec. 29th to 30th. In camp. Drew 3 days rations to last 5.

Dec. 31st. Moved 16 miles.

1865

Jan. 1st. Moved to Elk River. 2 ½ miles.

Jan. 2nd. In camp.

Jan. 3rd. Started at noon and marched to Athens 11 miles. Two days rations drawn to last four.

Jan. 4th. Started at 7 a.m. and marched to Indian Creek 18 miles.

Jan. 5th. Started at 7 a.m. and marched to Huntsville 7 miles and went into camp and laid off camp ground.

Jan. 6th. Rainy. Worked on our shanties.

Jan. 7th. Fine day.

Jan. 8th. Fair.

Jan. 9th. Rainy.

Jan. 10th. Changeable.

Jan. 11th. Raw winds.

Jan. 12th. Fair.

Jan. 13th. Fair.

Jan. 14th. Pleasant.

Jan. 15th to 20th. Pleasant weather.

Jan. 21st and 22nd. Rainy.

Jan. 23rd. Freezing.

Jan. 24th to 29th. Cold but fair weather.

Jan. 30th. Presentation of a sword to Lieut. Colonel Erastus N. Bates gotten up [*sic*] by the 80th Illinois.

Feb. 1st. Pleasant.

Feb. 2nd. T.J. Williams and C. Harris started home on furlough.

Feb. 3rd to 5th. Pleasant.

Feb. 5th to 8th. Changeable.

Feb. 8th. Snowed.

Feb. 9th to 15th. Changeable.

Feb. 16th. Pleasant. Gen. Grose took command of the 1st Division and Col. Bennett took command of the 3rd brigade.

Feb. 17th. Pleasant. Had brigade drill.

Feb. 18th. Pleasant. Had brigade drill.

Feb. 19th. Fair.

Feb. 20th. Had drill preparatory to remove.

Feb. 21st. Fair.

Feb. 22nd to Mar. 2nd. Changeable.

Mar. 2nd. Our division review.

Mar. 3rd to 12th. Changeable. Considerable rain.

Mar. 13th. Had orders to be ready to march at 7 a.m. Marched to the depot and got on the cars and went by rail to Knoxville. One car of our train ran off the track and killed one Lieutenant and wounded 21 men, 2 of them seriously.

Mar. 14th. Arrived at Knoxville at 3 a.m. and moved about 1 mile northwest of town and went into camp.

Mar. 15th. Left camp at noon and marched 9 miles and then camped for the night.

Mar. 16th. Marched 6 miles through the rain and mud and went in camp 1 ½ miles west of Strawberry Plains. We got two recruits.

Mar. 17th. In camp. Weather pleasant.

Mar. 18th. In camp. Weather pleasant.

Mar. 19th. Weather pleasant.

Mar. 20th. Pleasant.

Mar. 21st. Rain. Seroy [?] came up.

Mar. 22nd. Pleasant.

Mar. 23rd to 24th. In camp. Weather cool.

Mar. 25th. Left camp at 8 a.m. and marched to [*illegible*] Creek 16 miles.

Mar. 26th. Left camp at 6 a.m. and marched to Russelville 19 miles. Roads good. One recruit came to the company, John Underbrink. Passed through Morristown.

Mar. 27th. Left camp at 8 a.m. and marched to Rogersville Junction 6 miles.

Mar. 28th. Left camp at 8 a.m. and marched to Shields Mill 8 miles. Fixed up quarters and built good shanties. Camped in a swamp.

Mar. 29th. In camp.

Mar. 30th. The 80th and 75th Illinois were detailed to clear off the railroad track. We took the rails and ties off the track as far as Midway Station. Had considerable rain.

Mar. 31st. Our Colonel selected out another campground. We went to the new camp and fixed up our quarters.

Apr. 1st. Moved camp early in the morning and then fixed to march. Drew rations and then marched to Greenville.

Apr. 2nd. In camp. The wagon was sent back for our knapsacks.

Apr. 3rd. In camp. Our Colonel sent a squad of rebel deserters back to Shields Mills. Received news of the fall of Richmond and Petersburg.

Apr. 4th. Our baggage came up and we also got 5 day rations. Third division came up and went in camp here.

Apr. 5th. In camp. One brigade of the 3rd division moved out.

Apr. 6th. Moved camp. Camped near the depot.

Apr. 7th and 8th. In camp.

Apr. 9th. In camp. Preaching in all the churches in town.

Apr. 10th. Received news of the surrender of Gen. Lee's army.

Apr. 11th. The 1st brigade passed through here going back to Shields Mill. W. Edwards came to the company.

Apr. 12th. Rainy. William Diamond came up.

Apr. 13th. Pleasant.

Apr. 14th. Pleasant. Fired a hundred rounds in memory of the surrender of Gen. Lee and his army. Had services in all the churches in town. The town was illuminated.

Apr. 15th. Rainy. Received news of the assassination of President Lincoln and Secretary Seward.

Apr. 16th. Pleasant. Lincoln's and Seward's assassination confirmed. [*In fact, Seward was severely injured but was not assassinated. He survived the attempt on his life.*]

Apr. 17th. Pleasant.

Apr. 18th. Left camp at half past 6 a.m. and marched to Rogersville Junction 19 miles. We joined our brigade at Shields Mill. Weather rainy.

Apr. 19th. In camp.

Apr. 20th. In camp.

Apr. 21st. Went to the depot at daylight and got on the cars and started out at 9 a.m. Arrived at Knoxville at sundown and laid there until 11 p.m.

Apr. 22nd. Arrived at Chattanooga at 3:45 pm. and left at 5:45 p.m.

Apr. 23rd. Arrived at Nashville at 1 p.m. We got our dinners and then moved to our camp ground.

Apr. 24th. Fixed up camp. The 9th, 30th and 84th Indiana, 77th Pennsylvania, and 75th Illinois came in. Colonel E.N. Bates went home on furlough.

Apr. 25th. The 84th Illinois came up. Weather pleasant.

Apr. 26th and 27th. In camp.

Apr. 28th. In camp. Rainy.

Apr. 29th. In camp. Pleasant.

Apr. 30th. In camp. Mustered.

May 1st. In camp.

May 2nd to 3rd. In camp. Warm and pleasant.

May 4th. William H. Clayton died. Weather warm.

May 5th. Drew rations. Warm.

May 6th. Abraham Sherfy took sick. Warm.

May 7th. Warm.

May 8th. Rainy. Put off review.

May 9th. Gen. Stanley review the 4th Corps.

May 10th. In camp. Drew rations and put up a tent to hold meeting in.

May 11th. Rainy and cool.

May 12th. Pleasant. There was a torchlight procession.

May 13th. Warm. E.C. Thorp went to Tullahoma. Col. Bates got back.

May 14th. Received news of the capture of Jeff Davis.

May 15th. Pleasant, drew rations. The men got up a torchlight procession and went over to Corps. headquarters.

May 16th. Warm. Inspected by brigade inspector in the evening. We got up a torchlight procession and went to Gen. Stanley's Hd. Qtrs. Short speeches by Gen. Stanley and others.

May 17th. Rainy.

May 18th. Showery.

May 19th. Rainy.

May 20th. Warm.

May 21st. Warm and showery.

May 22nd. Pleasant.

May 23rd and 24th. Pleasant.

May 25th. Rainy. Gen. Grose got back and took command of the brigade. He was honored in the evening by a torchlight procession. He and Col. Bennett made short speeches.

May 26th. Pleasant.

May 27th. Pleasant. Capt. Wright came up.

May 28th and 29th. In camp. Weather warm.

May 30th. In camp. Weather warm.

June 1st. In camp. Warm.

June 2nd. In camp and warm.

June 3rd. Commenced making out muster rolls.

June 4th to 7th. Worked on muster out rolls.

June 8th and 9th. Examined and corrected the rolls.

June 10th. Mustered out of the U.S. service. Left camp at half past 12 p.m. and got on the cars in Nashville at 4 p.m.

June 11th. Arrived in Louisville at half past 11 p.m. Got dinner at the soldiers' home. We then crossed over to Jeffersonville and got on the cars at 4 p.m. Arrived at Indianapolis at half past 11. Laid here until half past 6 the next morning.

June 12th. Got on the cars at half past 6 and arrived at Lafayette at 12m [*noon*]. Left Lafayette for Springfield at 12 p.m. [*midnight*]. Arrived at Camp Butler at 3 the next morning.

June 13th. Arrived at Camp Butler. Went in camp southeast of the barracks. Rained from 6 to 10 a.m. The 85th Illinois came in.

June 14th. Capt. Wright came up with the rolls. The rolls were examined by the paymaster and sent out to be signed. The 80th and 81st turned over their arms and accoutrements. Drew rations. The 101st Illinois arrived at Camp Butler.

June 15th. In camp. Signed the pay rolls. Williams and Culp went home.

June 16th. In camp. The 84th Illinois was paid off.

June 17th. Turned over our camp garrison equipment. Williams and Culp came back.

Appendix

Report of the Adjutant General of the State of Illinois (1900-1902)

The Eightieth Infantry Illinois Volunteers was organized at Centralia, Ill., in August 1862, by Colonel T.G. Allen, and mustered into United States service August 25, 1862.

Ordered to Louisville, September 4, and was assigned to Thirty-third Brigade, Tenth Division, Army of the Ohio, Brigadier General Terrell commanding Brigade; Brigadier General Jackson commanding Division, and Brigadier General McCook commanding Corps.

October 1, under General Buell, marched in pursuit of Bragg, and, passing through Taylorville, Bloomfield and Mackville, was engaged in the battle of Perryville, October 8, losing 14 killed and 58 wounded, including Lieutenant Von Kemmel killed, Lieutenant Andrews mortally wounded, and Lieutenant Colonel Rodgers and Lieutenant Pace severely wounded. Generals Terrell and Jackson were also killed.

October 12, moved through Danville, Lebanon and New Market, to Mumfordsville. October 31 and November 26, made two marches to Cave City and returned. November 30, moved, via Glasgow and Hartsville, to Bledsoe Creek. December 26, started in pursuit of John Morgan, marching, via Scottsville and Glasgow, to Bear Wallow, arriving December 31.

January 2, 1863, having discontinued the pursuit of John Morgan, marched to Cave City, Bowling Green and Nashville, Tenn., January 8th, and Murfreesboro, January 10. Was assigned to the Fourteenth Army Corps, General J.J. Reynold's Division.

March 20, the Brigade, of 1,500 men and two pieces of Artillery, while on a scout was attacked by John Morgan and 5,000 of the enemy; but they were repulsed, with heavy loss.

April 7, moved to Nashville, and was assigned to Brigade of Colonel A.D. Streight, Fifty-first Indiana Volunteers. Brigade, consisting of Fifty-first and Seventy-third Indiana, Third Ohio, Eightieth Illinois, and two companies of Tennessee Cavalry, with two mountain howitzers, embarked, moving down the Cumberland and up the Tennessee Rivers, and landed at Eastport, Miss., April 19.

Marched to Tuscombia, where the Regiment was mounted. April 26, moved from Tuscombia. Were attacked at Dug's Gap and Sand Mountain, but, on both occasions repulsed the enemy, and, at Sand Mountain, captured a battery of two guns. Loss in the Regiment, 2 killed and 16 wounded. Captain E.R. Jones killed, Adjutant J.C. Jones mortally wounded, and Lieutenant Pavey severely wounded.

At Blunt's farm, May 2, again defeated the enemy, and, May 3, was surrendered to a vastly superior force, under General Forrest, who, contrary to stipulation, stole its blankets, watches and money. We were taken to Rome, and paroled and sent in coal cars to Atlanta. From this place the officers were sent to Libby prison. The enlisted men were sent, via Knoxville, Tenn. And Lynchburg, Va., to Richmond, arriving May 13, and thence to City Point, arriving at Annapolis May 17. On the 19th, moved to Camp Chase, O.

On June 23, having been declared exchanged, moved to St. Louis. 29th, moved to Nashville, Tenn., Lieutenant Herman Steincke taking command of the Regiment; Colonel T.G. Allen having resigned and Lieutenant Colonel A.F. Rodgers and Major E.N. Bates being prisoners of war.

September 8, moved to Stevenson, Ala. Captain Cunningham taking command. October 16, moved to Battle Creek, Tenn. 23d, marched to Bridgeport, and reported to Colonel Hecker; Third Division, General Carl Shurz. On 27th, moved up Lookout Valley, and was present at the battle of Wauhatchie

November 24 and 25, was engaged in the battle of Mission Ridge.

On the 29th, commenced march to Knoxville, Tenn., reaching Louisville, 14 miles from Knoxville, December 5. Longstreet having retreated, the command returned, arriving at Lookout Valley December 17. This march was made without wagons, tents or baggage, and rations were forged from the country. The command suffered from want of clothing and shoes.

On the 24th of December, was assigned to Third Brigade, Colonel William Grose, Thirty-sixth Indiana; First Division, General D.S. Stanley; Fourth Corps, Major General Gordon Granger Commanding.

January 27, 1864, moved from Whiteside, via Chattanooga and Cleveland, to Charleston, Tenn., and thence to Blue Springs.

Appendix

May 3, 1864, commenced the Atlanta Campaign. Participated in the battles of Dalton, Resaca, Adairsville, Cassville, Dallas, Pine Mountain, Kenesaw Mountain, Marietta, Peach Tree Creek, Atlanta, Jonesboro and Lovejoy Station. During the campaign, the Regiment captured about 150 prisoners, and lost 25 killed and 60 wounded.

Camped at Atlanta, September 9. Marched October 3, in pursuit of Hood, to Allatoona, and via Kingston, to Rome; thence to Galesville, Ala.; thence, via Alpine, Fayette, and Rossville, to Chattanooga, arriving October 30. Moved to Athens, Ala., and to Pulaski, Tenn. 23d of November, commenced falling back to Nashville.

December 15 and 16, participated in the battle of Nashville, and captured a three gun battery and 100 prisoners. January 5, arrived at Huntsville, Ala. 7th, Major E.N. Bates, having returned, assumed command.

March 12, moved to Knoxville, Tenn.; thence to Bull's Gap and Shields' Mill, March 28. Moved to Greenville, April 1, and from thence returned to Nashville.

June 10, 1865, mustered out of service, and proceeded to Camp Butler, Ill., for final pay and discharge.

Only four of the captured officers ever returned to the Regiment. The remainder being held as prisoners until March 1, 1865, when they were paroled for exchange.

The Eightieth has traveled 6,000 miles, and have been in over 20 battles.